DYING TO SURVIVE

DYING
TO
SURVIVE

by Carolyn Stoloff

DOUBLEDAY & COMPANY, INC.

GARDEN CITY, NEW YORK

1973

Grateful acknowledgment is made by the author to the editors of the following magazines, where many of these poems first appeared, for permission to reprint.

"Leaving Their Faces Behind," "At Sea" first appeared in *The Michigan Quarterly Review;* "Under the Flame Tree," "The Seventh Day," "For an Electric Man," Part II, as "I Put on My Eyebrows," and "For an Electric Man," Part III, as "Of the Moon," in *Poetry Northwest,* Copyright © 1969 by University of Washington, "If a Goose Has Twenty-Five Thousand" in *Poetry Northwest,* Copyright © 1965 by University of Washington, "Looking Through Trees into Holes" in *Poetry Northwest,* Copyright © 1971 by University of Washington, "Acrobatics," "The Blizzard of Thirty-Six Hours," "Beyond the Zoo" in *Poetry Northwest,* Copyright © 1967 by University of Washington; "One Station at a Time" in *The Little Magazine,* Copyright © 1972 by The Little Magazine; "That Close," *The Beloit Poetry Journal,* Copyright © 1970 by The Beloit Poetry Journal, "Myself as a Harbor," *The Beloit Poetry Journal,* Copyright © 1971 by The Beloit Poetry Journal; "Every Apartment Faces a Pentagon" in *Invisible City;* "September Night" in *UT Review,* Copyright © 1972 by Duane Locke, "Brick by Brick," *UT Review,* Copyright © 1972 by Duane Locke; "The Poet," "Pictures," "Under the Sun" in *Carleton Miscellany;* "He's Packing I Hear" in *Hearse,* No. 14, Copyright © 1970 by Hearse Press; "Notes on an Early Room," *Equal Time;* "Looking for Buttons" in *Choice,* Copyright © 1970 by Choice Magazine, Inc.; "The Reading," "For an Electric Man," Part IV, as "After the Long Trains," in *Lotus* No. 1, Copyright © 1971 by Jonathan Hemley, "My Pole," "Travelling Man," *Lotus* No. 2, Copyright © 1971 by Jonathan Hemley, "My Senses," *Lotus* No. 3, Copyright © 1972 by Jonathan Hemley; "Odyssey of the Hair" in *Epoch,* Copyright © 1972 by Cornell University; "List" in *Poetry Review,* Copyright © 1967 by Duane Locke; "As the Hand Goes" in *The Miscellany,* Copyright © 1972 by Miscellany Organization; "Short Subjects" in *Kayak* No. 25, Copyright © 1971 by Kayak Books, Inc., "The Guardian," *Kayak,* No. 21, Copyright © 1970 by Kayak Books, Inc.; "Lazarus" in *The Antioch Review,* Copyright © 1957 by Antioch Review Incorporated; "The Image" in *The Dragonfly,* Copyright © 1972 by The Dragonfly; "Go, Search Diligently" in *Center,* Copyright © 1971 by Carol Bergé.

Thanks, too, to the National Council on the Arts and Carolyn Kizer for their generous encouragement.

FOR SONYA DORMAN

Contents

I

II

III

DYING TO SURVIVE

I

LEAVING THEIR FACES BEHIND

I know now why old people travel
they travel to leave their faces at home
faces they meet in mirrors of ocean liners
in Hong Kong hotels   in dress shops
on the Rue de la Paix   belong to passersby
old natives   not our travellers

Our travellers' faces look back at them
from fresh places   eyes filled with beginnings
flick and swirl in potholes of their skulls
smoothing out irregularities
accommodations are identical

But empty skulls suck up rain and sun
rivers of swarthy arms   plumes
fantastic foliage   its portholes of bone—
open to the flux of great oceans   have become
vacuum cleaners of the nations

Eyes grow dark with wonder in gypsy caves
souls become light-footed as adept
hands empty pockets of ballast
in the bureau mirror in Des Moines
a face gathers fine mist
like blooming varnish on old paintings

See the planeloads of wingless sparrows
deceived into weightlessness
nibble Earth's ripe berry
nourished they escape the fouled nest
setting their backs against the sunset

Children recognize them
they receive the new day with innocence
they are losing their last teeth

Nowadays old people travel
they are not confused
they leave their faces behind mirrors
in Abilene   Boise   Chicago

Their dresses and shirts drip
from shower curtain rods of the world
Haifa   Halifax   Brussels
their small change seeds pores
and sockets of ancient walls

AT SEA,

there is never a shortage of physicians
when they smell a queer fish
they are right there   ready to perform
without consultation they grab your line
and sever it   never mind
what you are attached to
you're a menace to the deep
if you have your own slant on things

When you give up cigarettes and go under
you are prey to ad libitum advice
I was a long way from my maiden trip
when a solicitous intern   a porgy   pressed
me against an old hull
and recommended an automatic pilot   by then
I was getting the hang of things   I unplugged
my radio and zigzagged into the current
happy as a lark

As I kept to windward of the Sanitation Facility
on Flushing Bay   floating garbage in the vast
unmade bed took on an exotic aspect
I felt the tug of the East
and coyly wiggling my belly approached
an attractive mackerel to take him in tow
but he was a physician and did not want to go
places   hmmmmm   I murmured as though the stethoscope
were already at my chest   I did my best
describing the clear sea   the purple algae
I am a brain surgeon he said simply
unsnapping his instrument case   I put on speed

I have been polishing my binnacle
and studying the charts for a short route
to Istanbul where   it is said
physicians are less scrupulous

THERE'S NO END TO IT

I

woman in movement can hold more wounds
than a high tree   more nests   more light
a continent may take place in her arms
the slaughter of thousands
her warriors who lost their heads
shoulder guns more dangerous than lust
cramming her bark with blood

II

unripe fruits bleed in ditches
where full breasts collect
like rolls after the gods' picnic
women leak wasted sperm

there's no end to it
missiles rub their bellies along highways
littered with skins
houses burn

dead fingers drag seaweed
through cities indifferent to disease
ingrown nails fester and break out
in plastic roses

III

when flesh nearest bone
hangs limp on clotheslines
waiting to be claimed
and stew reeks in ladles
of daughters who must also die
how will gouty generals
be hauled from their flight
towards the edge of the cosmos
back to the bladders they occupied
how will those now standing rise

COME LADS

come lads   comrades   come rage
sheep off to the limp aged war

dry-eyed dreary lords
ready you to die

come raid the not yet bled
dying them red them yellows

yelling your worried *whys*
alone in the fell deads hardly

bare numb boys   numbered
unhumaned   uni-formed

they won't ache your bullets
it's your war ready or nuts

you are their scrape guts
to be butched and roasted

led in rows to the war-b-cue
trimmed to concur to fire

some errors come and gone
were seasoned with Rosemaries

some sons crossed fall ways
men's eyes will never see

LEANING

Leaning against wooden bins
      against dresses swinging from rods above them
      leaning against empty dresses
Leaning against headless horses beside smoking holes
      horses that get you no place
      leaning against stiff horses that give
      like righteousness   not toppled but shifted
Leaning against the sound wall
      growling jets
      steady drops large as onions
      emptiness hammered in
      anguished farting and groaning
      as the crammed beast rises
Leaning against the hard hollow growth
      spreading on earth's skin
Leaning against this factory
      its crucial bird heart
      its electric lace
      its frantic metabolic hunger
I look to land that recedes like an ocean
      I look toward land

LET'S SMASH

plates first   their circularity
their stacked slick surfaces
shelves next
rectangular calls to order
burn them

release nightmares from boxes
where hair grows in darkness
we'll have strength
to topple the whole structure

disrobed for the ritual
you'll chew holes in my wants
spit my teeth on barren fields
wipe color from my dreams
as I   withholding secrets
murder our firstborn

wallpaper rots around us
children covered with scabs
roll in gutters of bombed villages
among bloody rags

flakes from your plaster fingers
will coat me as ash
coats itinerant monks
I will bless you in white
you will tickle me with daggers
until I swallow you

stripes trap us with awnings of illusion
decorate flags to rally round
bestow rank by profusion as we change sleeves
describe paths of forced marches

and rows   tombstone houses in suburbs
books   armies of them
bearing in charred letters
evidence of historic events
institutional columns to be torn up
by the roots like asparagus

but let's begin with the plates
they cannot hold our hunger
we'll devour each other
wolflike   from the dirt

UNDER THE FLAME TREE

Oh what a zoo, love, this continent between us
cross-country to the sea
fish jump in our bellies
a dusty rhino shakes his horns
at the embattled sky
no room to charge   around his island
oil slicks   our clotted wings

I have no scars on my arm
no knives climbing to heaven
beyond human hearing
I fly by you
by you searching my skin
not a sound

If I feel your breath at my ear again
if you come back
we will rest like holy cows under the flame tree

If you come it will be over heaps
of abandoned vehicles
through hospitals stripped of their beds
if you come back shedding stones
I will draw out my breastbone
to place in your unwrapped fingers
we will lie under the flame trees
where I search the debris
for your large hand left by a population
in flight   vanished   clutching
tickets for an impossible journey

I will read the typed notice tacked to the wall
after the long battle
keep the way open
and the rains will begin in earnest

MORNING COME

from behind black thistle
through bark   bleeding depth
riding resinous wind

morning   come

through night's leaking mouth
from frog-smelling palms
along souring passages

morning   come

to worms stretching and shrinking
to pockets   to pain
to pulsing rooms in bellies

morning   come

the buried cling to us
our unlit tongues
missing limbs itch

morning   come

to soldiers on one side
numbers on the other
rise dead men rise

come morning

THE SEVENTH DAY

The air trembles
its flesh crawls
trees behind it
tremble too
pine smells
sweet in the heat
its needles glisten
white in the light
a bird whistles
me clean

Sky blues
the mind blind
each grass
stalk bristles
the curve of this hill
rims my world   a bell
in a steeple tolls
for bare maples
but my time
is green

To steal honey
pick a way
through blackberry
you will find me
whole as God
in the light place
I have made
we will share
the Seventh Day and forget
as He did

A COAL IN MY POCKET

I confess to a seaport
and time: a coal in my pocket
hands hang limp here
green coins from elms
those that are left on grackle street
graze a crushed nestling
my feet shy from it
I walk while I wait
I meant to wait
mine is the third train

the sea was cold
cold as money
I screw my head in deeper
against wind
it comes from behind
lifting grey scales
on shells stained with coffee
abandoned by lace
one bitter summer

the news inks my hands
slaughter and theft
my uncut mineral hours
I treasure them   I burn them
children armed with laughter
skip through me
a dizziness of ragged tulips
blossoming toward the schoolyard

I've lost track
a nurse glides by on rubber feet
this way   this way   she calls
leaning into the wind
white sharks swim
to the church spire
a tooth slides down my shirt
somewhere the sea
rails along it

also the brick station
sturdy as a hospital
on the second floor
ghosts with red flags signal
as anywhere the horizon—
between tear duct
and the far corner
trains leave anyhow
I hear mine

IN FROM THE COLD

for M.T. who returned for a week

That day we went kerplunking in the snow
looped as a couple of calves
swearing we'd stay   if we slipped
in the gutter   leaning chin on hand
one knee up   singing quartets
until they came to take us
the beefy men with badges
whose bellies are stainless steel

She swore she'd protect me (my knight)
through fire   as natives loomed
blackening snow with their shadows
she, bitter wild loving as an acorn
yelled she was glad she'd left
sick as she was of them: pale females
stuffing slack infants in her ears
black boys dropping bags
knives tears all over her floor

Tired of the tug of both sides on her
who wanted just a pencil a brush
to speak or sing with   tough color:
ochre vermilion moss-green
yelled she was glad
glad she'd left   glad she'd swapped
greens for sauerkraut   and wept

That night the hungry year changed
downtown smelled of burnt Christmas trees
and the house of pork fat
insides greased, I felt like a full bottle
when war slipped in
took my hand humanly   its terror
its skin   smooth as a queen-nun's
and hanging apples banged my head wherever I turned
and my palm was filled with bleached almonds

IF A GOOSE HAS TWENTY-FIVE THOUSAND

If a goose has twenty-five thousand
muscles to control, explain me our posture.
Pillows stuffed with their flight are bolsters
to lean on when, weary with gain, we summon
wings to guide us through treacherous midlife.

Their facile migration mocks us by day
as we shuffle, skin to skin, with plans
to summer in Sweden or Greece. One
by one planes take off, promiscuous.

Chained to abundance, to agents who arrange
our trips, hoods of blue skies,
quaint pictures, we are bent on buying.
More than feathers on a bird, we have pills,

pages to leaf through, investments that flutter
and drop. Do you hear them knock
at your hearts, the geese, in insistent formations?
They lift men from the gutter as we stoop
calling for greater production, and a doctor.

ONE STATION AT A TIME

to be read to rock

Birds drop over the landscape
if I shot them I don't remember
I leave them for dogs with soft mouths
or let them sail away wounded
my friend you insist on business
but I'm not a businessman
I must take my trip my way
I take one station at a time

Now the road runs from my feet in black streams
so I take the train
silk fishbones collect in my palm
while I sleep   between stations
maybe a wounded duck drags its wing
across your desk   finish it off for me friend
I'm up the steps my ticket in my hand

I have torn the six thousand glass
pages of the directory in half
addresses and names litter the woods
children gather them on their way home
in the evening because I take rhymes
as they come and stations one by one

My friend, listen, the world cannot be
peeled or squeezed we cannot make a moebius
strip of it   my spider caught a virus
and lost its design so I take it easy
with a fist I commit crimes everyday
travelling the same line
I take one station at a time

Bridges sofas sheets fold behind me
before my eyes the ocean's scroll rolls up
my heart is a squirrel's heart
fed by children   a torn zinnia
my heart gives birth to a thousand worms
because I can't buy a round trip
because I take one station at a time

LAST SUMMER'S BONES

Before delirious children upset their bicycles and begin to spin
Before whales perfume our shore with their rotting mountains
and October wind devours oak leaves
weaving them into ambidextrous curtains
opening on operas in Berlin and Copenhagen

Before coins enter invading soldiers' gums with carniverous intention
and nurses' lips pucker around stones under the fruit trees
against beetle juice and feathering frost
Before our wool unravels and the mind's stained glass
cracks so the light floods us
Before builders cement angelic hands between firehouse bricks
as though the Bible were asbestos and the prophets' beards
could put out burning grass in the crotch of progress

Before entrances and exits become indistinguishable
I'll take your face between my knees
extracting its cemetery tooth by tooth
to renew the playground   its wrestlers
to water your blood with abdominal roses
to rekindle last summer's bones
the tips of our wild asparagus

CARROTS: THEIR MEANING AND USE

carrots may be munched as enemy bones
they may be sliced and served as noses
of earnest men who can't see beyond them
carrots may be fitted with wings and sent soaring

carrots may be peeled and boiled
to unresisting softness like middle-class children
they may be hidden in baskets and dropped
in the path of a conqueror

carrots may be fed to cavalry horses
whose speed and magnificence as they trample
crops of foreign fields
reflects the glory of our nation

REPORT ON THE TIMES

July 29, 1969

At nightfall fierce winds and floods beset us
rivers rose in Rome, London, Dresden
reports of sewer lines swept away
bridges collapsed   trapped motorists
three feet of water lapped Mainstreet
rain held down crowds at Nice
at Yosemite—flattened tents
campers swept into gullies

Rain washed out Egyptian positions
prisoners advanced through waterways
in Viet Nam one hundred and twenty
civilian dead blamed on the rain

Victory went to the Minnesota Twins
evidence pointed to rain
it pelted the Upper Nile and the Amazon
pelted Musial, Hoyt, Campanella
washed out the Hall of Fame game
in New York the Mayor was charged with collusion
other candidates promised a change
as meteorologists dragged the dead
from the Passaic, the Arno, the Seine

Rain restricted the need for weapons
threatened landslides and depressions
accidents left twelve million pregnant
economists cursed forecasters
and spawned theories blaming the rain
it was rumored astronauts returned to the moon
Earth was in quarantine

At midafternoon the President rose
stoically in the rain for the National Anthem
and promised a gradual reduction   soon

THAT CLOSE

It rains hard rain   the President's
lips collect it from the pane
as he welcomes moon rocks
voices   dry boots

my eyes open against rain

I drink silence   it tastes cool
it tastes crystal   it embosses a boot
on the gold coin in my forehead
a flag opens

the moon has come that close

I listen to the earth
brush pollen from my knees
lift jewelweeds grown chest-high
to see sky on wet myrtle

no wind on the moon

here, tongues protrude between
stones   oaks may be yanked up
wings hang   earth's soft dough
sticks to my fingers

the moon is behind the rain

translucent stalks break
through tar   mantises devour
foam on grass   a crane vomits
gravel behind a hill

on the moon it is still

EVERY APARTMENT FACES A PENTAGON

every apartment faces a pentagon
at 1 a.m. a mother shrieks at her son

this goes on all night
at 8 a.m. the window opens

his tusks shine in the sun
sometimes it rains

a neighbor clears his throat
he expectorates

he brushes his coat
and goes out

he walks a line
in his old raincoat

in the room where I eat my brains
it takes all day to keep clean

a voice announces the death of 200 men
I wipe my mouth

what are they talking about?
are the casualties theirs or ours?

a hole keeps turning in
on faces on limbs

in the pavement
in torsos washed by rain

in new guns
a dark hole

the Washington Monument is a horn
a toothbrush   a stone

all roads lead to the same building
the riddle is how to get

from one spot to another without
getting wet

SEPTEMBER NIGHT

1971

stones drop from the night
fists of generals who squeezed
more bones through death's gap
than death requested

soldiers with iron stars on their chests
shake empty sleeves
flesh drifts between trees
clouds   termites' nests

settles on a hat rim
beside gloves on foyer tables
under portraits
of closely shaved diplomats

drops   like a wet handkerchief
on a cook's forehead
she kneads
red dough in her dream

stones drop from the September night
shot from Roman slings
from cannon
the heat and flames where they fall

could bake a loaf

LOOKING THROUGH TREES INTO HOLES

Croton-on-Hudson

looking through trees into holes
into the Eden-wound   I see
rats slip through festering cities
hear promises fiddle air
like crickets on summer nights

looking through holes between masts
bent by wind   through what is clean
touchable   I hear motors erase evergreens
scoop gravel from streams
drill my ears

looking through holes as a child
world upside down   moon underfoot
wounds filling eyes with fall
leaf into blood   ink the calendar
one day burying another

looking through holes that focus today
in a box   into litter-flat news
looking into now's nothing   an empty gun
a trumpet of lilies
promising regeneration

looking into the lemon lily afternoon
beeing its sweet
carrying it to cities to strew
so gardens will grow again
in spaces between politicians

I see trunks of speechless men
climb into holes   into bone houses
babies rest on women's hips
sons stand on their fathers' shoulders
building temples   praised by women

the man-forest as holy and travel slow
to pick flowers with those who know
what to call them   cement out of sight
I see Earth   this thunder rock
sail   somehow   into light

AS THE HAND GOES

as the hand goes so goes the heart
the feet follow
hands do not play football
with heads of indigents
hands   the skeleton's lips
disclose sentiments and goals
by involuntary dances

if hands are caged
in the distance they reach
songs they sing sweep the country
wringing   clapping
hinging gates   hands tie
wishing knots in loose flesh
to keep it from slipping into the sea

hands are the arbiters between taking
and making   when they join
mortise and tenon fit
and building begins again
the gift of a hand surpasses all gifts

a hand is the true water cup
though fire collects in the palm
a stove to the injured
long after feet fold
when backs are beyond bending
and mind
crumbles under the heavy step

hands are the soul's flowers
acquainted with earth
where lessons take root
in the Bible of the blind
creation is the width
of a finger tip

II

MYSELF AS A HARBOR

Heads rested on the rail
as the Pope in full panoply
was lowered into the sea
feet first in a plastic bag
when the inverted question mark
that supported him
hung again in its superior position
when the last miters had fallen
and lay like lobster claws
along the length of the quay
when lace rejoined spume
and red taffeta capes wrapped
around masts of untenanted sloops
as though the sky
had been nailed to a cross
and the bleeding sun were about
to walk on water   when gulls
skimmed the sea
for foul fish that surfaced
and bishops   naked now
I reached for a hand   darling
I breathed collecting six on my lap
where they crawled or paused
on the edge waving a digit
until gulls snatched them up
one by one
to crack on the breakers
snapping at fragments of meat
that sprayed in every direction
and I   left without lovers
sawed my west pier at the knee
from an outlook on the hill
wax tears fell continually
collecting in slippery deposits
until my emptied cranium
bumped down the incline
still the sun glazed thistles

on my breasts and belly
and a steamer or two entered my harbor
releasing sailors who tied
my limp neck cords
and fastened a sail over them
one can depend on seamen
monastic insular far-sighted
specialists in the anatomy of departure
they continue to bump hulls
against weathered thighs

FROM A SNAPSHOT OF THE POET

for Robert Peterson

a devil's brush in your lapel
but no jacket   near you a wheel

rusts against the wall you lean on
you write of trees birds and so on

I can't see them   there's no snow
to hide the planks and refuse now

in your whiskers an uncertain
mouth forms orange cats   ascertaining

quick hearts and delicate flutists
a philosopher's gentleness fresh

from the quest with clotted fur
and a voice sweet as a wire

chuckling across the continent
you pretend you're flat   arms bent

on your chest as though closing music
in   yet I have heard you dance

on the keys   and by chance
found your whiskers on certain peaks

THE POET

I   AS A BOY

the poet   as a boy
confesses love for   O'Neill
ready to be son   lover   ready to rob
his huge sorrow farm
his roads rolling between cut hay
stretched either side until the eye
closes   the mourning sound
his name makes   O'
Neill   hidden holes   burrows
blind fingers enter   first touching silver
light along rims

the poet's head falls   doll-like
on a robust breast   he cries
quietly for Hemingway's son
in contact with surfaces
no longer frantic

long hair clings to her bell-
body that answers him from beyond
the silent park
a discarded continent sealed in liquid
where the poet   as a boy
red-nosed   thick muffler wrapped thrice
around his neck   drags his sled
his sailing ship   a rat's skeleton
behind him   milk in his mouth

II   HE BEGINS TO BEGIN

sharp edges turn in his hands
sulphurous lamps edge his organs

his green monkey counts coins
lifts his lips   smiles

as though his organs turned
jokes on   he begins to move

wrapping water
around the waist   buckling it

he lifts a lariat from the saddle
swings it   catches wind

the wind   a large cowfish
drags him across his dry bed

he takes the best dancer's hand
begins to move space   enters

throws himself across it
like a nun into her wedding

III   HE PUTS WORDS TOGETHER
the poet advances   breasts
bud under his shirt
he draws particles to him
a string in solution

> he sees the General's head rise from his collar
> hears German shepherds snap and growl

the poet carries a dove and a bottle
he strolls moon valley
among golden grain
his cock on a thin lead

> he sees the General's chest imbricated
> with medals glow in the night sky

the poet listens   sleep mats his hair
his feet graze wheat heads
a fish slides by at eye level
he feels a nose at the back of his knees

> the poet sees a peasant and wife holding hands
> by a cottage door   a gegenschein in the eastern sky

the poet wears an eel at his waist
foam escapes his massive lips
his hay-colored hair is smooth as cornsilk
bees drone in the valley

        he sees a black man with one ear to his shoulder
        stand on air   hears the shark's flesh and bones

the poet forgets his cock and with that hand
takes a begging bowl from his chest
stars rain into it
he eats them one by one

HE'S PACKING I HEAR

I exposed myself at dawn in his cadillac
the trees recognized us   his beard
my braid were the talk of the place
delivery boys left eyes on the porch
rustlings *might* have been deer

Skilled as a marionette master
he pulled strings from above
thought himself Priapus
his spoon simply mislaid   I grieved
under him   felt his tug
as a dog would   wished he could
as he boomed our news
into the credibility gap

Like a call from a drowning man
my name rang   he declared
his vulnerability in a roar
the mechanized guests wished to ignore
so smiled past as martinis were passed
and they stitched the lawn with startings
and stoppings   hair fell from my heart

He's packing I hear
the sound nibbles my ear
in my thigh a wood thrush
begins whistling
he has frankfurter lips
his waist's thick as a mattress
but I want him back
my throat's a clogged drain
my columns crack

I have no redress   he's leaving
without leaving me an address or a publisher
he's packing my papa into his luggage
scratching me from his skin like a milk stain
the homely old lion won't make me laugh again

Listen!   over the hill
he's packing my pelvis in his grip
like a new salad bowl
and my hair   a switch
to remember me by
to swat fruit flies
he's weighing my melons
before he stuffs them in
I must begin   I must
begin to grow out and up again

YEARS AFTER

even when his hand no longer
rested on her arm   the woman
transparent as an x ray
would open the door
to fall against his starched shirt

years after   her knee worked
against closed drawers
scented with lavender
where limp thighs lay
without tides or breath

he claimed it was the nuts
in the couch cushions
the squirrels twitching their tails
bees buzzing against the landscape
barks echoing in the court
her long neck like a finger pointing
the pale sprouts on her onions
made him nervous

at the hour of painted turtles
when ant eggs rustled in the box
and the orange skin uncoiled
under the sink   the scar broke free
and began to squirm

she would open the bedroom door
and see grey bearded men
squatting along brown roads
and his letter   glistening
on the desk
under the lamplight

NOTES ON AN EARLY ROOM

shoots prospered in my humid room
pods split   God shot out   whiskered

each hair tipped with a pollen crumb
mother pitted me   she insisted

I use virtue as wallpaper
and organized sins in button boxes

yet fruits prospered and split   seeds
peppered the floor like rabbit droppings

mother scratched behind God's ears despite
the competition   they retired

rain came   vines stuffed my bureau drawers
and crawled over me choking sleep

honeysuckle dusted the place   I sneezed
and sneezed   I sizzled in sneezes

even she could not contain them
or the boredom that thistled my skin

stains told my story: snot and tears
mother tucked me under her arm

and brought me to the desert to learn
the law   I have grown dry wandering

RADIANT DOLDRUMS

wind arrows from the sea
surround the tan brick building
where my commodious grandmother
scattered crumbs on her sill to gather
brown twitterings as her bodice
collected pins   their heads shone
the way home to her vast merriment
her irises   shaded by ptotic lids
snapped light back like water
puckering over an immense content

grandmother crocheted this midi-blouse
for a doll lost on a long beach
blue with rose edging, it rests
in my palm   a calm geometry   each stitch
actual as a master's sketch
wind can't blow everywhere at once
this contact with her generous hands
nearly drowned by forty showering Aprils
becalms me at her still point

MY MOTHER

On Fourteenth Street   broad   without people
my mother's face gleamed against cluttered
windows   beautiful   yes   a real
poached egg   very delicate   she keeps
to cashmere even in August

She cleans vegetables cleaner than anyone
my mother cooks stewed chicken and chicken soup
and flounder   cotton-white in its own
pale jelly   my mother specializes
she takes full credit

When she has time   next week maybe
she'll carve ceremonials   people
who rise so high in their own estimation
they almost fall   unique segments linked
tenuously like ants on end   my mother
builds temples with her hands

Yes her little white hands used to startle
the living room with arpeggios
with a shivering motion from the shoulder
she shook off droplets before she raised them
and they splashed into Jeux D'Eau

Because of rain and windchimes in the alley
I see my mother smiling   her long lips
do delicate angular things instinctively—
jugglers   playing around after hours
sometimes with father's words
flicking them back disguised

When not amused the far ends of her mouth
jerk up on strings   but she does not rise
swiftly from smooth linens   her fine laces
rest in the sideboard   for who
would launder laces like those these days

LOOKING FOR BUTTONS

Who cares what buttons the old woman chooses
she may choose my eyes from the bowl of water
if they surface like sick fish
if they swell into fists tight as plums

I plunge my eyes in the bowl of water
my hairs make their way in the earth
who cares if an old woman chooses ivory
buttons for her shabby coat or a boy picks

them to kick with his thumb in a mock
serious game   once you drop them in the well
by the bed you no longer write any rules
if not they will go to the river in a sack

I drop them in a bowl by the bed to sweeten
corridors of my body   I put them aside
as I would two avocado seeds while my brain
sprouts a rootless fern but the city's

a nail that ticks in the foot of sleep
its static invades the wireless
                              a persistent cough

THE READING

At dinner my lost leg was served to me;
my head, a Pompeiian portrait, collected light.

During the recitation the sunset, on which a pale
moon was pinned, collided with opacity.

Suffering heat loss, plagued by scratches,
in spite of a second blanket of smoke, I saw

my voice, my lower arm. The reception
was immaculate. In the library an eye closed.

The matador, become monumental,
raised his cape against the Evening Star

as Monadnock's profile receded
into a luminous horizon.

But this morning the verdict came—
a mailbox stuffed with grass.

I wrote a passionate letter.
I could do nothing less.

THE COW

She has seen the celandine
gleam in the dark
summer upon summer
and the farmer take calves
to be slaughtered
and the barn swallow raise her brood
twilight   pierced with swallows
snapping food from thin air
as she pursues her thankless task
tasting the same cud   what flops
in the trough
bloodless as grass
field to stall
barn to field
an octopus at her teats
rubber and gleaming steel   and lo
what more is there
than the taste of her nose
but the bull   his staff full
and hard under her tail

FOR AN ELECTRIC MAN

I

hands full of bulbs
that don't grow   but light

flexed against fat   against bronze plaques
screwed in to secure a man

you pause with catalogues
in worn armchairs

between brown walls
with women around who eat roast male

                          •   •

rising to a long muscle on the horizon
you dress   watch sky through glass

climb till it escapes your mouth
morning   cloud women   open

poise counts where you   high   unfold
stretch wire   turn on

bridges so they glow   a gift
you forget how it began   at what age

II

I put on my eyebrows and went walking
among gigantic bees over water
between grey uniformed sentinels
at precise intervals to find you
financial towers reared their profits
on the askew graph of cables
beneath me docks balanced
on black velvet fingers   warehouses—
absorbing their blindness

in a tobacco-stained hammock
over the river souls of corrupt
and corpulent politicians swayed

dreaming green birds   I could not see
the moon of my nail   and where
were you old hedge leaper? I looked
among red flags and high wires
for gull-colored hair   for your slim
form to slip its key in the wind

III

of the moon four slices had been removed
only a luminous crucifix glowed

when I came to you through the carpeted halls
when I took you to your window

it had become a sign with little bulbs
that blinked on and off as it moved

across and very close to the glass
it told the temperature   the time

of night too   our heads touched
as though we shared a childhood secret

I remember the way we unfolded across the bed
I the explorer   found hills and plains wider

wilder than home   but the fountain of my youth
was not to be found

the hotel had been given five stars
yet your eyes   no deeper than wallpaper

did not see me or my fleet
we shared no common tongue

and the cost of the journey!
I had come halfway round to find myself

on cracked pavement with broken toys
a charred ball among them

IV

                    after the long
trains turned on their sides
from time to time a scared eye
appeared at my door   a flower, dumb
in the grey earth of your face
                    I stood firm
sucked down the drain, your ring
stuck in scum and phlegm   cut hair
caught on hooks linemen climbed
as telephone poles flicked by
                    nail parings
scraps of reason in the trash
could be picked out by any witch
behind me in the sea   laughing girls
touched each other's breasts
                    a gong boomed
your memory cast in bronze   *what
can be bought with a penny?* my fingers
cried   while the murderer sat
behind bars of venetian blinds
                    studying circuits

BRICK BY BRICK

you descend the subway
with clean socks
and your lunchbox
watch the landscape: your face
in the window
a masked epiphany

welder, your rough palms
slipped into my skin   I'm aflame
with white chrysanthemums

I walk the hard week
with fur slippers
in my chest goldfinches flutter
to be released
in city streets
on my birthday

when   oh when
will the rooms be open
for habitation

I've a brick for a pillow
sirens measure
the distance between rivets
when will our vines light
when will raised arms of statues
drop   and children
buried to their chins   rise

when will a beating yolk
climb the sky
and the house be ready

MY BALD HEAD REFLECTS

I used my last hairs to darn my socks
now my bald head sings light back
bongs against iron sides
swung by the late hour

my pear-shaped head   carunculous
reddened by sun to the color of lungs
holds the earth   its worms
rotting pages dropped by trees

blind spinners of theologies
sensual insects that drag whale-
sized lovers through tunnels
to feed young incubi

my head   bald as an egg   splits
wet-feathered muscles squirm through
to rooster the world awake
retreat to a bone world   a ruined Thebes

this skull   with HUMAN hammered in
wound running with pus   with pleasure
reflects the sun   suspended
the fixed pit burning in empty fruit

oh bare head   empty as a pit
large and little as an O among numbers

DYING OF IT

Sparred with you on the fifth level
and the fourth
murdered you on the sixth
found peace
chest to chest never dead
though dying of it
toward silt
at the lake's bottom
carried you through sky
you lifted me too

At 3 a.m. Thursday
from a bed that swelled and sank
my reality
as sparrows chirped
brash unstrung
beads from the thread of us
we strolled out of me
with no palms to cup rice bowls
no trap or prison left
or soiled faces at skylights

ATTEMPTING TO MAKE LYRICS OF MY LOVERS

Attempting to make lyrics of my lovers
I disassemble them with a razor
and handling their parts tenderly with white gloves
hang them among the leaves
arranging and rearranging

This provides me with entertainment for many days
and birds with nesting material
if they succeed in stealing a hair
as I lean over the microscope
to examine attachments of ear to scalp
in order to part them with surgical precision

Let those unscrupulous winged reptiles
collect what they will for their shelters
their records   cut from the same mold
go *tweet tweet   seraph seraph*
where are you?   tuning up
for a symphony that never begins

I shall compose operas when I reassemble the parts
even now I catch choruses of surging crowds
coronations   shouts of victorious entry
seductive refrains cloaked in hallucinatory richness
scraps of them glow
amidst the monotonous summer foliage

Let the birds construct according to blueprint
let them fiddle the tunes appropriate to their species
for occasionally from the throat of a thrush
comes a short passage of such linear perfection
that my razor slips and a new organ
shapes itself in my hands

ODYSSEY OF THE HAIR

one of your hairs entered my mouth and lodged in my throat
so I sing of your pale body stretched on a plastic beach chair

by a sea of cigarette butts and pistachio shells
under a bruised sky

I sing of boxes and envelopes holding love scars
bait to catch angels spawned in electric light bulbs

I sing of your baby mice fingers
of your neon tongue announcing films that flash in the orrery:

you as the constellation Bear wearing earphones
as the Crab in a red suit of sin

you—the Lone Ranger   stiff in hand
to thrust up the anus of a supermarket

as the goat crunching cars in which tyrants stand waving
as the giant fish that swallowed the cock of Osiris

you—scattered across the celestial sphere
that turns 10 degrees nightly driven by discontent and denial

one of your hairs entered my esophagus   sped down the rapids
with a week's supply of canned music

explored the rain forest   sliced through veins
until the ruined capitol rose in the clearing

entered a labyrinth of slaughtered kings whose bones
glow on the shelves like noctilucent eels

one of your hairs broke the clay seal to the sanctuary
repainted the goddess   clothed her in soiled sheets

and the sun rose like a cloud from the crushed glass
and the desert of flesh bloomed with androgenous trumpets

LIST

a gnat on the white of a drying sheet
a seated letter in a complete Webster's
a nerve end sensitive to wind
a cast in the eye of a crystal sphere

one sparrow peck   a "son of" in the lists
of Genesis   in Seurat's masterpiece La
                Grande Jatte
a dot of paint   a small complaint
from any alive man dying to survive

a tight bud in the floods of spring
a spine of feather in a Peruvian cloth
any interruption of the blue by bird
                You
buried in the cold cash of the world

ACROBATICS

One last push,—I'm up!
At the buffet they mill and chew
as I strain to maintain altitude.
Look, look! I gasp.
Heads tip, jaws drop.

Frappé, frappé, sur le cou de pied,
balancé, balancé, glissade, changé.
I leap to display my sublime elevation
and repeat the routine:
ta ta TA, ta ta TA.
They shut their mouths on the caviar.

Dizzy from splendid postures
with which I delighted air
I fall, fumbling with the string.
The wings will not open.
The professor sits, lips pursed
legs and arms crossed, eyes fixed
on a distant star.

MY POLE

A wreckage   framed   hung over my head
silver leaves wilted   keys
dropped through my fingers like broken glass
the clock's hands
reached for me in my armchair

Rat regiments moved in from the west
became a cavalry
crusading against closed houses
pounding hoofs raised dust around me
the stench of hair and hide

I grabbed my pole   let the world
jostle and jolt I cried
I have hold of my scraps   I am a child
it is May   the colored ribbons
connect at the top

III

WATER TO WATER

The shapes a head makes of words
swim in deep water
a bowlful in a room of fish

In the hand a breast becomes
a field of wheat in eaten bread
a smooth stone in a palm

Knock on the bowl
mirrors begin to tilt
holes errupt

Eggs crack   remain whole
as   rich with fish
water returns to water

BLACK BLUE OR YELLOW

look! my hands are crimson
beyond the window—sky
red as a boiled lobster
and in the bowl the eye's
bloody pulp

snow-bite on the tongue
haunts me   also
a sick man's skin
mud under the nails
and hyacinths: a blue scent
flowering in my lungs

no shadows   only a stain
the color of dark roses
a glowing coal in the sky
with never a black
night's peace

I set out   hectic
a banner stitched
with the holy language
blowing in my skull
hacking through chokecherries
I pursue the blue the yellow

I SEE THREE FISH IN THE BOWL OF WATER

fish one could be fish two could be fish three
is fish one *fish* to fish one and so on
is fish one *fish* to fish two et cetera
they know no not water
so no water
fish, fish, fish, fish, fish, fish, fish in the not sea no water

there is a boat on the sea
the water the keel cuts through
there is a boat on the sea they say
the boat *is* if it is *on* the sea
is the boat where they said—on the sea
if I do not see it
if I saw it would it be
if deck under foot I did not see it
the boat no other than my felt feet and the sea not
both less than they said it

when I see the sea I will see less
than the sea they said entirely

is my arm to me if I do not see it arm necessarily
if I do is my am's arm the arm I see
arm I see when you say arm more arm is
than the arm on me

fish fish fish from the sea
in the net in the hand of the arm
of me who less is than the whom you see
when they say human   but to whom

ON THE TRAIN

I sit on the seat and the train moves
the train moves the station rushes by
the poles rush by and the trees
a house further out slips to my right
hills swim leisurely at the bottom of the sky

If I walk to the rear of the car
for a cup of water
if the train moves at forty miles an hour
at what speed will I rush
to my destination backward as I walk
to the rear where the water is

The earth moves under the train
which way does it spin on its axis

The earth unhung circles the sun
with me on the train
smaller than a grain

UNLESS THESE OBJECTS WERE ALL MINIATURES

The miniature bottle at eye level
which contains a crystal
is only slightly smaller than the vase
half hidden by two rectangular solids
in the painting by Morandi
pictured on the postcard
propped on the shelf below

the painting must be larger than this picture of it
but when I hold the miniature bottle close to my eye
it is four times as large as the vase
in the reproduction of the painting by Morandi

unless these painted objects were all miniatures
which could be
because we don't see where the table ends

on the other hand
the surface on which they rest
being exactly the color of white sand
under an overcast sky on a bright day
which is not white
they could be a monumental grouping in a desert

which swells the miniature bottle with the crystal
that can't be shook out through the bottleneck
and I become gigantic   so large the tight onionskins
of reality appear as separate shelves

THE PLANT ON MY TABLE HAD SEVEN LEAVES

the plant on my table had seven leaves
it has twenty
it also has nine and sixteen leaves

the plant has no leaves at all and its stem is diseased
the plant with its withered stem is outside my door
it is on the piano and has thirty-one leaves

I don't have a piano
I have a plant
it's on your table

well it's there
it's not at all like this plant yet
it happens to have a white plastic pot

or: the plastic pot has a plant in it
one leaf has a brown edge
except for that leaf the leaves point upward

it is not a philodendron
it was a philodendron for a second there
as you see each leaf has dark green spots

I don't know the exact size
parts of some leaves are hidden
each leaf is larger and smaller

one can say with certainty each leaf
is smaller than the whole plant
however the whole plant is smaller

the reason for this is there isn't any plant
though there is one
it's yours

SOUND ARITHMETIC

take a hole hanging from a tree
put "pear" into it
when the ripe pear falls
pick the hole and eat it
when you feel full
throw the core away
there will be a pear hole hanging
and a whole pear where it fell
that's a pair of pears
and the pear you ate makes three
and the pear hole on the core makes one more
so you have four pears
that's eight

take the core with the hole of the pear you ate on it
and slip it in the pear hole on the tree
so the two fit exactly
now pick the pear that fell up
and put it back
that makes one pear
you ate one
that leaves one

DOORS AND KEYS

the hall door didn't close
none of the doors have keys he said
I just wanted to shut the door
the outer door closed
the door to my room never closed properly

last night on coming home
I had trouble finding my key
I asked about the lock on the door
I wanted the door to open

none of the doors have keys he said
is there a lock on the door I asked
yes he said   softly
many homes don't have doors I said
yes he said   and closed one

he left the other door open
I closed it

CONCERNING THE IDEA OF VASE

VASE: an open thing
it has an opening I mean
what we call vase is where it's closed
though what the opening opens into
the hollow it is full of
makes its vaseness

VASE: what can contain
flowers for instance
or weeds or whatever fits
the size made tall or wide
by how much of what
you put inside

It could be trees
instead of flowers
or the Eiffel Tower

CHAIR

what is so simple as a chair
upright   palpable   open

I join it note by note
a breathing accommodation

when I walk from here to there
I will see the chair I sat on

the future is like that
irrevocable but separate

SHORT SUBJECTS

I   TO CATCH A CLOUD

begin with an unruffled lake
wait for a cloud to pass over
see the cloud in the lake
reach down   pinch the lake's
skin between thumb and forefinger
raise it as you would a silk
handkerchief   the cloud will stick
put it in your pocket

II   SOUVENIR

begin with the Yangtze
you are on it watching sampans
an orange sunset
stand   without rocking the boat
reach as high as you can
grip a corner in each hand
and peel down to your feet

write a message on the back
stamp and mail

III   LOGIC

begin with a feather picked up
on a walk in Vermont or Central Park
glue it to paper
draw a bird around it

claim your bird has flown

IV   RETRIBUTION I

begin with an empty cup
take it by the ear and shake it
turn it upside down on the saucer
knock on the bottom with a spoon

when you hear a hiss
lift the lid and let one escape

keep the others as hostages

V   RETRIBUTION II

paint an elephant on a plain
a few miles away

with tweezers transfer
to your enemy's ear

VI   RECIPE FOR CATCHING DRAGONS

heat wire white hot
knot a net with it

if you can do that
you don't need a net

WHEN LONELY

take your hand from your pocket
hold it in the breeze
let the stars swarm to it

let the divorced night
dickering for a settlement
creep between liver and lungs

draw with your right hand
the black hump of a mountain
there are lovers pressed into it

remove a pair
and put them on the sill
still corked to each other

draw your head in
and close the window

AT THE APPOINTED TIME

At the appointed time
the clock's gears stop
gliding a drop stops
a thrusting man
briefcase in hand stops
a butterfly in a train's
path stops it   clouds
stop behind the cloth
of a woman wiping glass
an echo stops midway
the roller coaster stops
just over the top
the reel stops the swimmer
drowning at the appointed
hour   he breathes

MY BONNARD

Eyes full of his eyes or mind's eye image
or brush-in-hand's image-making
choice of vermilion invented around
beneath green sea grapes, paint grapes, rounds
surfaced by hand's choice moving in time
his time, him
full of color of his place, mirrored,
placed, doublerich by time he took
and color he put on plane, surfaced
sieved to see through to his
hand, paint, and making
recognized as having been made, as he saw
in that time and place, permanent, thing
out or in, there, where he was
now here, on eyelids, red as after grass
in brain, grapes, green as after vermilion.

PICTURES

I IN THE OVER-EXPOSED PHOTO

In the over-exposed photo
one can just distinguish the man
freckled with sun
from terrace stones   leaves
the blazing news he holds

his mind exists in the ink
in the sudden twitch
soldiers make as they drop
he sits at his terrace edge
with dying men until light

eats this snapshot

II PREPARATION FOR PORTRAITURE

When she combs her hair coins
fall into palms of dark men drawn
to the dusk under her skylight
on which faces
hardening like starfish   wait
to appear in place of pears
she brushes without breaking skin

pears soften on tables on chairs
making moist places in dust
she practices
form with them as theories slip
through her brain
theories on how wars begin   named
for the most beautiful   Helen sleeps

a cloth over the face that now
appears on each painted pear

UNDER THE SUN

How the sun shines today
a man can hardly look at it
a man who walks on wet
sand at the rim of the sea
feels very small under the sky
near the immense body
that spreads and shrinks
waving like a blue flounder
feels very small on
the broad tan spine
the packed slick sand
on which his own sun shatters
reforming in liquid skin
a brilliant shield just beyond
reach a few feet
always a few feet before him
illusion! so will this moment go
a man thinks of Van Gogh's
wheat field   crows
under a spinning sun
down the beach his friend
small as a beetle on end
sees his sun preceding him
that makes three suns
every man who walks by the sea
under the sun has one
he can't seize to take home
a sun no one but he sees
where he sees it
the sun in the sky is at ten
o'clock   he calls to his friend
down the beach who turns

a man smiles   hand cupped
to hold something up

in the photo he lifts
a white hot light
that will outlast him

EXERCISE: TO HOPE TO INVITE
TO CONTINUE

Before he left me he saw me
he spoke to me before he left
I am happy to see you here he said
there was something between the eyes
that threatened to continue
before he left me he saw me
he said I love you

I hope to know
I want to understand
I will go for a walk
I can sit down
I don't want to go
I prefer to walk

Before he sat down I stood up
when he took the book I laughed
when he kissed me I sat down
he invited me to play
I hoped to know
I wanted to understand

On his way to the table
he found the apple
he did not want the apple
he did not want to be eaten
he did not want to begin
before going out he put on his gloves

As I came toward him I smiled
having taken the book he laughed
he began to write with a pen
I began washing my hands
he invited me to play
but there was something between the eyes
he said I love you   goodby

IV

LAZARUS

I ran into Lazarus when skin-diving
off the coast of Spain

lying with lobsters, he foamed in his beard
because he wanted to die

and couldn't (believing in Jesus as he did)
I felt real bad

about it of course   but what could I do
running out of breath

I nodded my condolences and left
him wringing his hands

THE CAPTAIN CHOOSES

The captain must choose between rocks and oranges
or be throttled by wires in the plunging engine.
He chooses oranges.
He will squeeze them in imitation of the Emperor,
an act of condolence.
He will peel them and throw the rind to gulls,
an act of charity.
He will, in an act of science, penetrate them
with his finger.
He will pile them, pyramid, and ascend to God.
He will build a house of oranges.
He will roll them among rooted feet at board meetings
and sing in sweet revolution.
He will hold them up before blackboards
demonstrating Earth's trajectory.
He will carry them in his clothes:
symbols of fecundity.
Tossing seeds, he will prophesy, in their conjunctions,
the dreamed woman, her exploding skin.

THE GUARDIAN

He did not want the bird's death.
He loved the bird.
He dreams the gritty slap of feet, the weight
the bird threw from perch to perch
until the cage bounced on its spring,
seeds crackling, struggles with cuttlebone,
the jerk of the yellow head tugging a bar.
He unhooks the porcelain water bowl.
Empty.

He dreams the room—a white immensity
against which colors sing.
Morning comes.
He draws off the cloth.
Escaped?
No, a yellow patch on the spotted
sandpaper floor.
Too late.
He reaches for a cigarette.

He leaves the room in which he was born
and travels by train.
At one station or another he removes
the stiff bird, examines the dry bowl.
He recalls pushing a finger
through the bars, remembers angry cheeps,
fluffed up feathers.
Gates open in the night.

The gate of the cage rises.
A large white hand reaches in
for a bird with legs
brittle as winter twigs.
He removes his hand and takes out a cigarette,
fearful in the face of dryness, of snow.
At night he returns to the room in his mother's house.
Still cool, he pulls covers over his head.
He coughs. A white hand lifts
the gate of his skull.

THE BLIZZARD OF THIRTY-SIX HOURS

I

Torn, it shredded, fragmented the shovelled
walked on hard below lookers in cages, beyond sellers,
or outside, where, blizzarded in its smell, sweet as cold,
weathered shoppers there to be out, not
knowing what scent, stockings, belted to put on,
clipped to the hearing, or shade of red
to speak from they wanted, walked,
or called to fourwheelers already full
of wish to be tucked ins not
having been forced out but drawn
by the blizzard, its each sheeting new, continuous,
soft silence to penetrate, to track now's emptiness
past into, as boxed watchers unfamiliar with checked
accumulation of wind, inching hand's passage,
moving cribbed up as any other fogged luminosity
would have done them, or low number,
who not outing to meet it not slipping on arm warmer
chest muffler, wall of cloth with window or long
hollow foot against wet, moved about in their own
central chill, hidden against it all,
against such a thirty-six hours.

II

Surrounded by its continual foliage, its fall,
in which fragments relate as rags to an ideal sheet,
as two suggest one that releases two, three,
four, a millennium of particles,
accepting its bed
as an unnamed river that is not
except full, or other than its changing filler,
not the earth's street
not the walls of buildings but space,
thick as an empty glove, reversed, holds the hand
it held, holding the hole

without end or beginning, full
of empty to be snowed into, house
holding it out in the stuffed brain of us,
its shreds of cold, white,
useless against red blood, we hear them laugh,
bitten out there, believing they know the snow.

MY SENSES

My eyesight has not improved. I can't see my loved ones across the room. They *are* there, they must be, nodding, smiling, elders' hands on shoulders of small sons who stand straight and wave, as though from a great distance. I wear glasses on my breasts to provide insights. I project what I like without them.

My nose has never been more acute. I smell burnt toast, urine, my own sweat. I smell individuals in a sum, their expectations, their lusts. Short circuits reek like bad onions. I turn, catch the door as it swings back. As a result of this facility I spend time on trains. On trains folks, once settled down, slough off odors which cling, a fine mist, to their windows.

I bite my tongue but I can't shake my taste. It runs to beautiful cousins whom I perceive through my nipples. I salivate. I should be ashamed. I drool over Persian eyes, cleft chins, profound voices tasty as baked ham.

My touch—now that's where I shine. I can caress a cheek without breaking skin. I can stroke a calf till it's meek. When it comes to touch the world kneels to me. Stroke after stroke they drop, friends, drummers. Stones rise where they have fallen.

BEYOND THE ZOO

On an occasional Sunday in spring or autumn, clothed in my librarian's gloves, I visited the zoo to hold out palmfuls of crackerjacks to the llamas and white tail deer.

In the dark it seemed important to hold on to the crushed crackers, but it was a mystery to both of us (myself, the giraffe), how, in my search among dusty velvets in the storeroom of the theater, I found myself with a full fist.

Surprise, a meager word for the effect on me of his appearance: luminous, dignified. On a small scale with a soft nose, something of the sort could have occurred without tangling the cables. This was unhoped for. A flame rushed through my limbs.

"All this," I breathed, "to one with so little cash. And they don't travel well."

Perhaps this was the dividend from my judicious investments.

I looked sharp. No, it was not a camel. A camel is a father, a giraffe is a chapel, and a more unbundled beast would be difficult to imagine, though, like the rest of us, a giraffe has a pit, or a stone, in the middle.

Oh I would have lifted him from the track of his presence to tuck in my nest pocket, or swallowed his length into the cage of my pelvis stuffed with straw so they could not bleach the spots or send him to college, but he was too tall.

Would he permit me to reach up and hug a thigh?

Slowly I opened my fist and stretched out an open hand with the crumbs from my neighbor's lunch.

But my gift was not leaves.

I have placed on the short horns of his shadow a veil of fine lace. I leave his unknown name in the prayers of my church, remembering a sunrise cannot be possessed, remembering he could have killed me with a kick.

THE IMAGE

Just leave yourself open, I said to myself, leave yourself open and tread water; throw out nets, be conscious of the rhythms of ground swells overlapping, aware of agitation, migrations, under the ruffled surface. Throw out nets and the world will throw back lines baited with shining flies. Catch as catch can, Carolyn, I said.

Leave yourself open, go clear and clean as a glass-bottomed boat observing urchins and cucumbers, sergeant majors and angels; go along trailing your net and small miracles of synthesis are likely to take place. Today, in that spirit, I went out.

I had not gone twenty-five yards into the park when two missal-ferrying nuns, two young women in medieval widows' weeds, hove into view holding down one red and one green balloon. That stopped me. An image! a TWIN image. A vision, a significant sign. It was even exotic. I crept up. I held out my glass jar. I waited. I clapped on the top.

But synthesis has not occurred. A whole sea, full of flotsam and jetsam, and they haven't made a single connection. As far as they're concerned they are heading southwest toward the 59th Street exit holding missals and the strings of one red and one green balloon.

Walking around with somebody's breath in a rubber bag stretched to the bursting point, walking it through the sky as it strains on its string toward the edge of the atmosphere, the empty places of the universe, as a dog strains toward a fragrant tail, takes a kind of raw courage.

They may have stopped to sit on their balloons by this time. No, insular, insouciant, they go about their business, stubbing their toes on the glass, each grasping her missal and a string. Round and round. Round and round.

What do they eat I wonder. I should have picked leaves from trees in the vicinity. I should have dug up a section of asphalt under them. Here I have two rare specimens and I am obliged to sit by twiddling my pencil as they shrink and dry like a couple of run-of-the-mill men.

What could be less inspiring than a leaky balloon. What could be less uplifting than a breathless balloon, limp and shrivelled, on the floor of a mayonnaise jar, to say nothing of a couple of youngish nuns walking, less and less buoyantly, cranky with hunger, toward their salvation. Already I'm losing interest.

The cyclists now, a more common lot—sardine types—coming, going,—all those wheels—connected with children, in-laws—on holiday from advertising copy and peddling insurance. Peddling. Pedalling up, coasting down—all sorts of ramifications. Take the ordinary and make *it* significant, I always say. And I let them get away!

GO, SEARCH DILIGENTLY

The message read: GO, SEARCH DILIGENTLY FOR THE YOUNG CHILD.

Obediently he hoisted himself on his horse and hastened to the East to rummage among ivy towers where he turned up an early Mozart manuscript in the guest room of a professor, a Viennese refugee, and carefully calculated the length and weight of the phallus on the scale in the niche beside the doorway at Pompeii, aided by certain occult documents and a remarkable Roman of his acquaintance. He was commended for his scholarship but discovered no Child.

Forced back by the Atlantic and his own erudition, he heeded the imperative "Go West, young man!" and proceeded to Phoenix where they were busy dying in comfort, ignorant of the prophetic book to a surprising lack of degrees. He distributed the book lists he brought with him and left cold desert nights behind.

Screwing the telescope into the lens, he climbed the Hollywood hills and followed, in rapid succession, several promising stars who did not lead him to the Child, but, by devious routes, back to his room where he confronted the same face across the court, the same old hand, the same tweezers. As though plucked eyebrows could make a Mary of that one!

Anxious to rejoice, eager even, he resorted to good deeds:

February 17—Saved his mother from an Irishman who swept the corridors.

February 18—Rushed to his mother's rescue at night when she swallowed a fly.

February 19—Composed a letter to the Mayor revealing the exact location of a dangerous hole in the pavement.

And so on.

He learned. No one could say he did not learn. In bed, he kept his mouth closed and one eye open for the angel.

During the next period, his brown period, he tried herding sheep, thus gaining access to likely stables without cost or the tedium of queuing up. Progress, definite progress, was in the wind as he celebrated his arrival, without serious scars, at the age of fifty. *Just follow the scent to success,* he murmured to his champagne glass. But it soon became clear he was allergic to fleece and dogs did it better.

Enough of that! Putting his blue crease-resistant trousers over his grey slacks, choosing, after painful meditation, a striped and a flowered tie from his extensive collection and knotting them neatly, side by side, at his throat, slipping his gold corduroy jacket over his navy blue blazer, his uncle's only slightly worn vicuna under his own checked overcoat, with his bag of gifts underarm, he left his room and threw the key away, committing its location carefully to memory.

He had some fine gifts to place at the Child's feet: a handsome vase with breasts and thighs purchased in Sicily, for instance; a few bottles of Ma Griffe, Chagrin and Faim; ancient coins from the Orient with elegant ciphers in relief, with square holes in the center into which the Child could fit pegs to prove his identity, and a white silk cope embroidered with gold, only slightly tarnished, which, over the years, he had even learned to decline: I cope, you cope, he copes—.

But to no avail. He recovered his key and locked himself in.

Behold! he exclaims to himself, *Behold!* thus keeping in trim for the big night.

Quite far-sighted now, he rests in his cradle. He can just make out terrible angles from whom there is no appeal as they casually gesture on the courthouse roof.

But as yet no Child. No child at all.

BECAUSE I HAVE SEEN HIM

I had just caught the ripe vowels shaped by his tongue, when the manager cracked his whip and our conveyance moved on.

Passengers, eyes closed, watched private movies of foreign wars. As we advanced through mountains, pacified armies shrouded us from the hot sun. Neither bark nor stones bled, yet I shouted: *Let me out! Let me out!* and returned to the smog banks and the poet on his high stool in the midst of traffic.

He was gone.

In the square empty brown bags escaped from men's knees as they lifted their faces to sun, and jets cast shadows over them.

Urn sellers ran fingers down ledgers and shook their heads.

In a warehouse I picked a way through mattresses to question the matron who measures. How long had it been?

Letters chattered, carriages slammed, horns bellowed, the city shook. I did not weaken.

Leaving my umbrella behind, I entered the night. Among victims and assassins, in crumbling districts, ambulances came and went. Policemen with shining whistles spilled from buildings stuffed with fur. By the dim light, on a factory wall, I read: LAY OFF.

No.

Tomorrow I'll take my slingshot and aim for the hawk among sparrows.

WHO COULD BELIEVE IT

If it had been shells, only shells, the recipe called for, instead of
yolks and madonnas, I could have stepped over the threshold with bread
in my hand to build your muscles with meals protean and consubstantial.
It would have been I, my preparing fingers, feeding your currents,
hoisting you up high ladders, along cables, to the highest bridge tower.
Shirt tails flapping in the wind, above smog and brokers, you would
have balanced on the brink of your assumption.

But you warned me against assumptions. "I am ruthless with
women," you said, tenderly stroking my thigh. Who could believe it?
Boys in white disappeared into cool choirs. Steeples rose. We swung from
them.

You would not deny your mother. How could you. At fifteen
your father stepped aside. Only the kitchen door stood between myth
and mineral. You placed coins in her hand.

Night after night your sister and she conspired against the
enemy, protecting their bellies with folded arms. But it was she, only
she, who recalled cupping your buttocks in one palm as she lifted
your full weight toward the ceiling.

There were auguries. I had my binoculars. Your nature could
be observed from a rooftop; departing birds too, slightly smiling.

Your eyes moved from brick to brick to elude meaning; you
continued to slap your knees and laugh boisterously at diners where
even the guests carried napkins on their arms; you entered the subway
at the regular hour with clean socks and your lunch zipped together,
as the packing proceeded.

But I'll linger in the station with my measuring cup, until the
last minute when you reach down to pull up the steps.

TRAVELLING MAN

As a boy, stretched over Maine coast on a rock licked black, he cast his petitions into foaming surf that tossed them back, shredded. Barnacles broke out on his chest. Between icy water and isolation he was forced to move on.

He travelled by bus to the Midwest where he stood in a field among speechless, cloth-wrapped ears, among plainness, potatoes, with no one to listen, not even a pine. This was worse than Maine.

In Mississippi they made him king. Ladies stroked him in effigy. He was encouraged to gambol and gamble. He was encouraged to take a wife and reproduce himself. He was respected because of the egg on his head; because, politely, he kept it intact, well-balanced. But the yolk became heavy and the ladies hung limp on his arms.

On a Thursday, his birthday, he caught a train to the Southwest where the saguaros made him feel young but vulnerable. Forced to make his way through prickly and unfamiliar wilderness, he became his own man. In Tucson, a dry tank for the dying, boots and spurs were permitted, and his horse, smart about thorns, could be relied on. Seeing the Z of his shadow on the animal's back, he concluded he would not grow up to be a cowboy of note, but at least would move with alacrity toward the splendor of his sunset.

Because sunsets, unlike postcards, remained out of reach, he kept travelling. When he saw the sea unstretch, he unstrapped his pack and whacked the beast's rump. So this was the other end! Same water. Negroes too. They carried blue strips of paper and moved on small wheels with few spokes.

He placed a protest call to the President to reveal certain patterns that had become clear to him. But the President, showering, could not hear him for the waterfall, and failed to return the call when he had shaken the water from his ears. Discouraged, the travelling man put his hands in his pockets and grew a beard. Wherever one went on this island it was the same thing.

Scribbling a note, he shut his mouth on it, hoping to float until he reached the mainland.

SUITCASES

Once again I found myself beside the three suitcases. This time they were neatly pyramided with papa on bottom and baby on top. I had only two hands. The train would be leaving at any moment from the station behind the stand of trees to my left.

We were on a side of the hill, a conical omphalus, whose peak corresponded to the center of the island. I would have liked to turn my back to them, to rush down the slope and into the sea, but for obscure reasons having to do with delicate health I had not been taught to swim.

The train, departing from the station, hooted.

It seemed, as I stood there uncertainly, I had stood there uncertainly for some time. It seemed, as I experienced a squeezing of the lungs which invariably accompanied the departure of a train or boat I could have taken, that I had experienced this squeezing of the lungs at this place some hours or days before. I therefore concluded that the train made a circuit of the island, and that, if I waited patiently, it would return. Then I would be ready and would jump aboard with my one suitcase or two.

The possibilities, after all, were not unlimited: there were three covering one suitcase only, and three combinations: mamma and papa, mamma and baby, papa and baby. I could arbitrarily predetermine a formula for selection, the top two for instance, or the two that would best balance, but under the circumstances neither of these formulas would be truly arbitrary. I could—my head ached.

I would open them *all!* spread dresses and shells, slippers and oriental rugs, address books and television tubes on the burnt grass, carefully select only necessities from each to pack tightly in the largest suitcase, distribute the remains in the other two for the sake of order, privacy, and to avoid the fine for littering and indecent exposure. I would abandon them. Yes, I must abandon them or be myself abandoned as cumbersome, indecisive, and incapable of travel; be abandoned in abandonment by letting go. I must let go, be wanton, travel by train to no specified destination so as to arrive continually, moment by moment; so as to leave continually though stationary at any and every point.

Perhaps it should be the smallest one.

I found myself, to my disgust, quite unwilling to give up any of the mysterious contents of this battered, anonymous blue bag. It held, if I remembered correctly, the secrets of darkness and some few stars. There were also pine forests, fields of tall dry grasses and goldenrod alive with the vibrations of wings and the rasp of chitinous legs. Was there among them any item of sound, sight or sense I would part with to make room for mother's or father's articles of apparel, treasured appurtenances of appearance and disappearance, keys to commodes and file cabinets, keys to locks whose cylinders had long since closed their keyholes and departed? There was my mother's Pierce Arrow, for instance, my mother's mother's sister's gold-leafed grand piano, the gambling casino at French Lick Springs with red tulip glass fixtures and a turmoil of glittering crowds. There was my father's straw hat, his brother's carnation, the trolley that passed their house. There were antimacassars and a glass-bellied case of knickknacks, the contents of attics, the accumulations of two lifetimes, reduced in size according to year and value, each detail preserved precisely as riggings and fittings on museum models of famous sailing vessels, and, even smaller, hand-me-downs of still earlier generations.

If only a vagrant would pass by. He could carry off one, two, or even three of these burdensome suitcases, and welcome. Charitably I would let him choose. I would leave it to him, to fate, no more arbitrary in the end than any decision, and catch the train with what is left to me, to memory, until the next time.

Hooting, the train arrived.

DATE DUE

PRINTED IN U.S.A